PSYCHOLOGY GUIDE

RADHIKA SHARMA

Contents

Preface

This book has designed to give a systematic overview to the readers about human psychology. Essentially, psychology helps people in large part because it can explain why people act the way they do. With this kind of professional insight, a psychologist can help people improve their decision making, stress management and behavior based on understanding past behavior to better predict future behavior.

Careers in clinical and counseling psychology are expected to grow especially fast due to the greater demand for clinical and counseling psychologists in hospitals, mental health centers, and social service agencies.

Psychology

Psychology is the <u>scientific</u> study of <u>mind</u> and <u>behavior</u>. Psychology includes the study of <u>conscious</u> and <u>unconscious</u> phenomena, including <u>feelings</u> and <u>thoughts</u>. It is an academic discipline of immense scope, crossing the boundaries between the <u>natural</u> and <u>social sciences</u>. Psychologists seek an understanding of the <u>emergent</u> properties of <u>brains</u>, linking the discipline to <u>neuroscience</u>. As social scientists, psychologists aim to understand the behavior of individuals and groups. A professional practitioner or researcher involved in the discipline is called a <u>psychologist</u>. Some psychologists can also be classified as <u>behavioral</u> or <u>cognitive scientists</u>. Some psychologists attempt to understand the role of mental functions in individual and <u>social behavior</u>. Others explore the <u>physiological</u> and <u>neurobiological</u> processes that underlie cognitive functions and behaviors.

Psychologists are involved in research on <u>perception</u>, <u>cognition</u>, <u>attention</u>, <u>emotion</u>, <u>intelligence</u>, <u>subjective experiences</u>, <u>motivation</u>, <u>brain functioning</u>, and <u>personality</u>. Psychologists' interests extend to <u>interpersonal relationships</u>, <u>psychological resilience</u>, <u>family resilience</u>, and other areas within <u>social psychology</u>. They also consider the unconscious mind. Research psychologists employ <u>empirical methods</u> to infer <u>causal</u> and <u>correlational</u> relationships between psychosocial <u>variables</u>. Some, but not all, <u>clinical</u> and <u>counseling</u> psychologists rely on <u>symbolic interpretation</u>.

While psychological knowledge is often applied to the assessment and treatment of mental health problems, it is also directed towards understanding and solving problems in several spheres of human activity. By many accounts, psychology ultimately aims to benefit society. Many psychologists are involved in some kind of therapeutic role, practicing <u>psychotherapy</u> in clinical, counseling, or <u>school</u> settings. Other psychologists conduct scientific research on a wide range of topics related to mental processes and behavior. Typically the latter group of psychologists work in academic settings (e.g., universities, medical schools, or hospitals). Another group of psychologists is employed in <u>industrial and</u>

organizational settings. Yet others are involved in work on human development, aging, sports, health, forensic science, education, and the media.

In 1890, William James defined *psychology* as "the science of mental life, both of its phenomena and their conditions. This definition enjoyed widespread currency for decades. However, this meaning was contested, notably by radical behaviorists such as John B. Watson, who in 1913 asserted that the discipline is a "natural science," the theoretical goal of which "is the prediction and control of behavior. Since James defined "psychology", the term more strongly implicates scientific experimentation. Folk psychology refers to ordinary people's, as contrasted with psychology professionals', understanding of the mental states and behaviors of people.

Early practitioners of experimental psychology distinguished themselves from parapsychology, which in the late nineteenth century enjoyed popularity (including the interest of scholars such as William James). Some people considered parapsychology to be part of "psychology." Parapsychology, hypnotism, and psychism were major topics at the early International Congresses. But students of these fields were eventually ostracized, and more or less banished from the Congress in 1900–1905. Parapsychology persisted for a time at Imperial University in Japan, with publications such as *Clairvoyance and Thoughtography* by Tomokichi Fukurai, but it was mostly shunned by 1913. As a discipline, psychology has long sought to fend off accusations that it is a "soft" science. Philosopher of science Thomas Kuhn's 1962 critique implied psychology overall was in a pre-paradigm state, lacking agreement on the type of overarching theory found in mature sciences such as chemistry and physics. Because some areas of psychology rely on research methods such as surveys and questionnaires, critics asserted that psychology is not an objective science. Skeptics have suggested that personality, thinking, and emotion cannot be directly measured and are often inferred from subjective self-reports, which may be problematic. Experimental psychologists have devised a variety of ways to indirectly measure these elusive phenomenological entities. Divisions still exist within the field, with some psychologists more oriented towards the unique experiences of individual humans, which cannot be understood only as data points within a larger population. Critics inside and outside the field have argued that mainstream psychology has become increasingly dominated by a "cult of empiricism," which limits the scope of research because investigators restrict themselves to methods derived from the physical science. Feminist critiques have argued that claims to scientific objectivity obscure the values and agenda of (historically) mostly male researchers. Jean Grimshaw, for example, argues that mainstream psychological research has advanced a patriarchal agenda through its efforts to control behavior.

You always find a problem.

It is psychologically normal for you to find another problem upon resolving one. One research demonstrated that volunteers who are asked to select computer-generated faces that look threatening eventually resorted to faces that do not. It turns out that as the volunteers ran out of threatening-looking faces, they started turning to faces that they would usually call harmless.

Why do we do the things we do? Why do some people like hot chocolate while others prefer coffee? Why do some live to surf while others would rather stay home and read a book? How can some of us put a name to every single person we've ever met while others struggle even to remember our own telephone number? Why do some people always seem happy and successful while others see no choice but to end their painful lives in suicide? These are the sorts of questions we can try to answer through **psychology**: the science of human behavior. In this short article, we'll briefly explore the different branches of psychology and get a quick overview of the kinds of things psychologists do.

What are the different kinds of psychology?

We can divide psychology into two big areas called experimental psychology and social psychology.

Experimental psychology uses classic, laboratory-based, scientific methods to study human behavior: it uses similar techniques to physics, chemistry, or biology, often carried out in a lab, except that instead of studying light rays, chemical reactions, or beetles, the experiments involve ourselves and other people.

Social psychology tends to study how people behave in real-world situations—for example, how people react to advertisements, why they commit crimes, and how we can work more efficiently in offices and factories. Social psychology doesn't always involve experiments; it might be based on questionnaires or observations instead.

Of course, we can study social psychology in a lab using rigorous experiments, just as we can carry out meticulous experiments in the real world; the division I've drawn between experimental and social psychology is arbitrary and artificial, but it reflects the ways in which psychology is often taught in schools and colleges, and how it's written up in textbooks and scientific papers. The reason for that is largely historical: in the late 19th-century, when psychology was still a very new field, psychologists were keen to be taken seriously as scientists, so they tried to adopt scientific methods to cloak the things they studied in respectability. To this day, there's a certain stigma attached to social psychology and sociology (the study of how individuals and groups behave in society); whether fairly or not, some people see them as soft science lacking academic rigor.

Branches of psychology

Humans are the most complex of all the animals, which explains why psychology is such a vast subject. Within the psychology department of a typical university, you'll find people working in a huge range of different areas. There are people who study perception (such as how our eyes and ears work), learning (how we develop as children and how we make sense of the world as adults), memory (why we remember and how we forget), language, thinking, and reasoning. While some psychologists study "normal" human behavior, others specialize in "abnormal" psychology, which includes how people behave when their brains are damaged or degenerate over time and what causes psychiatric disorders. Social psychologists study everything from the best way to design a <u>computer mouse</u> to whether we can really trust the evidence we get from people who witness <u>crimes</u>. Let's look at the various branches of psychology in turn, in a bit more detail.

Perception

You can think of people as living machines who receive information from the world, process it in various ways, and then act on it. In the mid-20 century, it was fashionable to talk about animals (including people) receiving a stimulus through their senses (maybe seeing a chocolate-chip cookie appearing in front of you), which then led to some kind of response (salivating and reaching out); according to a school of thought known as **behaviorism**, human behavior was all about the way a certain stimulus produced an appropriate response (and exactly what went on inside the brain to make the connection wasn't thought to be especially important: behaviorism was literally "mindless").

Since the 1960s and 1970s, psychologists have tended to view the human brain as a kind of <u>computer</u>, taking in information as "input," processing and storing it in various ways, and then producing "output" (some kind of visible behavior); this approach is known as **cognitive psychology** and we'll consider it again a little later. However you react to the world, your behavior usually starts with sensory perception: the way your five main senses (vision, hearing, smell, touch, and taste), plus other, lesser-known sensory abilities such as proprioception (your sense of where your limbs are and how your body is moving), feed information into your brain.

For most people, vision is easily the most important sense, closely followed by hearing; that also explains why perceptual psychologists have traditionally devoted most effort to studying vision, closely followed by hearing (comparatively speaking, the other senses have barely been explored at all). Most of us assume that we see with our eyes, but it's far more accurate to say that we see with our eyes *and* our brains. While we can't see without our eyes, it's also true that our brains carry out a huge amount of processing on the sensory impressions they receive—and in all kinds of interesting ways. One very obvious example is that we see things in three dimensions using separate, two-dimensional images that our brain fuses together from our two eyes. But we also see things based on what we expect to see, which is what causes most of the things we call **optical illusions**; for example, we see faces in clouds because our brains try to make sense of the world very quickly based on the things we've seen in the past (an awful lot of faces), the things we expect to see in the future (an awful lot more faces), and the things that matter most to us (the faces of people we love, work with, and have to interact with). We can get some idea of just how complex the human visual system is by considering how little progress computer scientists and robot engineers have made designing machines that can "see" in anything like the same way. Why are our own brains so good at seeing? It's (crudely) estimated that something like a third to a half of the cortex (the outer and, in evolutionary terms, "newest" part of the human brain) is devoted to vision. [2] That's a very impressive illustration of the sheer complexity of making sense of the world entirely by studying light rays that enter two big holes in your head.

Learning

One of the things that marks out humans from "lesser" creatures is our ability to make sense of our environment and learn from it. It's obviously untrue to suggest that humans are the only creatures that learn things: you can teach a chimpanzee to use a symbolic language, you can train a dog not to defecate on your carpet, a rat will quickly learn to run through a maze to reach a food reward, and even a simple sea-slug can learn a couple of basic tricks.

Learning goes hand-in-hand with survival, but it's a surprisingly large and complex subject. At one end of the spectrum, psychologists study the process of **conditioning**, which is how animals come to associate a particular stimulus with a certain response. One of the first people to look into this was Russian scientist <u>Ivan Pavlov</u> (1849–1936), who famously rang a bell when he delivered food to his dogs; eventually, he found the dogs would salivate simply when he rang the bell, even when there was no food around, because they'd been *conditioned* to associate salivating with the sound of the bell. When behaviorism was fashionable, some psychologists thought all kinds of complex human behavior might be broken down into patterns of stimulus and response. That's why, for example, you often see attempts to blame violence on TV and in the movies for wider violence in society. Now we know complex human behavior is much more than a simple knee-jerk reflex from stimulus to response.

One of the great things about psychology, which differentiates it from older sciences such as physics and chemistry, is that its relevance to everyday life is often more immediate and apparent. One branch of the psychology of learning is called **developmental psychology** and it concerns how babies develop into children and adults: for example, how they learn language, how they turn specific, concrete examples of things they see around them into much more general, abstract principles (the rules by which we have to live to survive), and the relative importance of "nature" (genetic factors—things we're born with) and "nurture" (environmental factors—things we're taught and learn). Developmental psychology has played a huge role in pedagogy and the scientific, theoretical approach to education; it's also a fascinating subject to study if you're a parent.

Cognitive psychology

Thousands of years ago, before humans started to create fixed settlements and developed agriculture, we lived much like other animals and day-to-day survival was our only preoccupation. How different things are now. Although the world's poorest people still experience life as a horrible daily battle to survive, most of us, thankfully, get to lead lives that alternate between (reasonably tolerable) work and (extremely tolerable) pleasure. Both of these things involve using our brains as much as or more than our bodies; both see us functioning as living computers—"human information processors"—that take in information, process or store it in our brains, and then output results. The way we process and store information is what cognitive psychologists study. How do we understand a simple sentence whispered into our ears? How can we remember everything from how to ride a <u>bicycle</u> to the names, in order, of all the American presidents? And is there any fundamental difference between these two types of memory (knowing how to do something, which is called **procedural memory**, and knowing facts about the world, which is **declarative memory**)?

Where behaviorists liked to pretend that "internal mental processes" didn't matter, didn't exist, or probably both, cognitive psychologists spend their time teasing out the precise nature of those processes, typically coming up with flowchart models that break such things as memory and language processing (a field of its known, often known as **psycholinguistics**) into sequences of discrete components. Applying this to the study of memory, for example, has given us models of mind that suggest memory breaks into separate long-term and short-term stores, with the short-term or "working" memory itself divided into distinct areas that process visual impressions, snippets of spoken language, and so on.

Cognitive psychology is not limited to how we process the structure of information, but also what information means. The word cognition is a synonym for thinking and reasoning, two areas that cognitive psychologists have also studied using computational models. How do we make informed decision making about things, such as whether one car is a better buy than another? Why do we live in absolute fear of things like terrorist attacks but happily cross roads, drive cars, ride bicycles, drink alcohol, or smoke cigarettes (all of which pose far greater risk to our safety and health)? Why do we play lotteries when the chances of winning are so much less than the odds of being struck by lightning? These are the sorts of questions cognitive psychologists consider under the broad umbrella of thinking and reasoning.

Intelligence

Though related to cognition, intelligence, which we might define as a general ability to solve problems, is a separate area of study, and it's much less fashionable than it used to be several decades ago. There are several reasons for this. From Sir Cyril Burt (a prominent British psychologist who allegedly faked research data about his studies of intelligence) to William Shockley (the co-inventor of the transistor who, predictably, became embroiled in controversy when he dared to suggest that there was a link between race and intelligence that made white people intellectually superior to blacks), the study of intelligence has often proved intensely controversial. The controversies, though important, distract from a much more fundamental difficulty: how should we define intelligence and is it even a meaningful concept? Some cynics have defined intelligence as the mere ability to pass intelligence tests, but although **psychometric testing** is as popular as ever in recruitment for jobs, intelligence tests are not, and never have been, a predictor of people's ability to live happy, worthwhile, successful lives.

Neuropsychology

When you study psychology, it's remarkably easy to forget that most of the cool and fascinating things you discover happen inside the brain—an apparently unremarkable organ often compared to "two fistfuls of porridge." Neuropsychology is all about figuring out how the brain is structured and how different parts of it have different functions. One extreme, early example of neuropsychology, known as phrenology, famously involved quack doctors claiming they could tell interesting things about someone's personality by feeling their skull for bumps. Although the idea seems risible today, the central idea of phrenology—that the brain is modular, with discrete regions having specialized functions—is now known to be essentially correct. [4] However, it's an unhelpful oversimplification to suggest, for example, that the right half of the brain is dreamily creative while the left half is clinically rational; for most of the things we do, many different parts of the brain are involved, either working in parallel or in complex serial circuits.

While neuropsychologists do study healthy, functioning brains, they also
devote a lot of their time to researching people whose brains have become
damaged through such things as head injuries, strokes, or degenerative
diseases like Alzheimer's. We can discover much about how things like
memory and language processing work by studying what people can no
longer do when specific areas of their brain are damaged or destroyed. In
the most spectacular cases, it's possible to find people with very localized
brain damage who can no longer do very specific things (for example,
recognizing faces or reading words); we can infer from this that the
damaged brain areas play a key role in whatever function has been
lost—and that helps us build up a map of which parts of the brain do what.

Abnormal psychology

People are hugely diverse and different—that's one of the things that
makes life interesting. While it's difficult to define "normal" behavior, it's
somewhat easier to point to examples of abnormal behavior, which is
harmful to people and those around them. Neuropsychological problems
following brain injuries are one example, but behavior can also become
abnormal for a wide variety of other reasons, which we might broadly
divide into behavioral, cognitive, and neurochemical/biological. Eating
disorders such as anorexia and bulimia are believed to be largely
behavioral and cognitive, for example: you might develop an eating
disorder if you convince yourself you're fat, after becoming obsessed with
skinny catwalk models. Illnesses such as Parkinson's disease are more to
do with neurochemistry and biology: Parkinson's is believed to occur
when nerve cells in the brain stop producing dopamine, an essential
chemical **neurotransmitter** that sends messages around the brain. [7]

Psychiatric disorders such as depression and schizophrenia are hugely
complex and still imperfectly understood. Depression can occur for many
different reasons, which might be behavioral (you feel nothing you do
makes any difference and become miserable through "learned
helplessness"), cognitive (you analyze the world around you in a way that

persistently makes you unhappy), neurochemical/biological (for one reason or another, the chemicals or the basic structure of your brain are geared to unhappiness), or some combination of these things. The study of schizophrenia has a fascinating history, with attempts to explain it shifting from anatomical/biological causes, through cognitive and behavioral ones, and back again. Originally described as a kind of premature dementia ("dementia praecox"), by the 1960s it was being painted (by such figures as R.D. Laing) as a kind of sane reaction to an insane world, and now it's much more likely to be considered a consequence of complex, interacting factors such as a person's particular genetic inheritance, life events, substance use, and brain chemistry. [8]

You'd think understanding the cause of a psychiatric problem would be the first step toward treating it but, remarkably, psychiatry has often worked in willful ignorance of what was happening in the mind, partly through the influence of behaviorism, partly through the challenge of anti-psychiatrists who refused to believe in what they called the "myth of mental illness," and also because the underlying causes of psychiatric problems were genuinely not known. Treatments for psychiatric disorders were largely doled out on the basis of what seemed to work and what didn't; if clinical trials found that drugs cured more depressive patients than, say, group therapy (talking about your problems with other patients), drugs became the treatment of choice. It didn't necessarily matter why they worked or how, providing the patients showed an improvement. That's how hugely controversial psychiatric treatments such as lobotomy (surgical removal or destruction of parts of the brain, also called leucotomy) and electroconvulsive therapy (electrical shocks to the brain) became popular in the mid-20th century. Just as psychology tried to cloak itself in experimental and scientific rigor, so 20th-century psychiatry latched onto the respectability of medicine, often masking a substantial ignorance of how and why disorders actually occurred. Today, thanks to advances in neurology, neuropsychology, and neurobiology, we have a much clearer understanding of how the brain works and why it can malfunction—but many questions remain.

Here are a few key milestones from the history of psychology and psychiatry over the last few hundred years.

- 1649: René Descartes draws a clear distinction between the mind and body—formulating the so-called "mind-body problem."
- 1802: Thomas Young outlines the first scientific theory of color vision, based on the perception of three colors red, green, and blue. His ideas are later elaborated by Hermann von Helmholtz.
- 1800–1850: Franz Joseph Gall and Johann Spurzheim found phrenology, a pseudo-science in which bumps on the head are taken to indicate the presence or absence of personality traits.
- 1860s–1870s: Paul Broca and Carl Wernicke kick-start neuropsychology when they identify regions of the brain (now named Broca's area and Wernicke's area) apparently responsible for language processing.
- 1890: William James publishes The Principles of Psychology, the first psychological textbook.
- 1900: Sigmund Freud's *Interpretation of Dreams* ushers in the hugely influential field of psychoanalysis.
- 1905: Ivan Pavlov carries out groundbreaking conditioning experiments with dogs.
- 1906: Alois Alzheimer delivers a lecture on the type of premature dementia now named Alzheimer's disease.
- 1913: J.B. Watson outlines the central ideas of behaviorism.
- 1923: Jean Piaget gives birth to developmental psychology with the publication of *The Language and Thought of the Child.*
- 1930s: Egas Moniz pioneers lobotomy as a surgical treatment for epilepsy.
- 1938: B.F Skinner advances behaviorism with his book *The Behavior of Organisms.*
- 1950: Raymond Cattell publishes a groundbreaking theory of human personality.
- 1953: Brenda Milner begins studying Henry Molaison (a patient known only as HM until his death in 2008), whose surgery for severe epilepsy leaves him with intact long-term memory but largely destroyed short-term memory.

- 1957: <u>Wilder Penfield</u> uses electrodes to map sensory and motor areas of the brain.
- 1959: <u>Noam Chomsky</u> delivers a blow to behaviorism with an influential attack on B.F. Skinner.
- 1960s: Anti psychiatrists such as <u>Thomas Szasz</u> (in the United States) and <u>R.D. Laing</u> (in the UK) question the very concept of (biologically based) mental illness.
- 1967: <u>Ulric Neisser</u> hastens the demise of behaviorism by publishing an influential book named *Cognitive Psychology*, which names, focuses, and energizes the cognitive revolution.
- 1970s–: The development of brain scanners revolutionizes neurology and neuropsychology.
- 1980s–: The marriage of cognitive psychology and neuropsychology produces the influential new field of cognitive neuropsychology.
- 1985: David Rumelhart and James McLelland publish a seminal two-volume book titled *Parallel Distributed Processing*, widely credited with renewing interest in cell-based (<u>neural network</u> or connectionist) models of the brain.
- 1987–: Prozac (fluoxetine) becomes a runaway success as a drug treatment for depression.
- 1980s/1990s: "Mirror neurons" (ones that recognize when animals see another creature doing the same thing) are popularized, prompting all sorts of new ways of thinking about social behavior.

How will psychology develop in future?

In the 150 years or so since psychology became a science, huge amounts have been discovered about why people behave as they do and how we can relate different aspects of human behavior to what goes on inside our heads. Even so, teasing out the many, remaining mysteries of the brain remains one of the last great challenges of science. Apart from being hugely interesting in its own right, another important prospect is the discovery of effective treatments for terrible degenerative diseases such as Parkinson's and Alzheimer's. A further interesting direction is the development of artificial intelligence, including computers and robots that can "think" and act in more humanlike ways. Will probing the mysteries of the mind help us perfect electro-mechanical rivals who make us obsolete? Or will the act of developing intelligent machines sharpen our sense of what it means to be human, making us happier and more fulfilled? Psychologists, you can be sure, will find the answer!

9 798887 725680